WOMAN

Author: Watson, A
Title: Woman
Publication Year: 2020
www.ashwatsonpoetry.com

Cover Artwork
Model: Laura Zella
Photographer: Isabella Mariana
Make-up Artist: Thairine Cordeiro

ISBN-13: 978-1-5272-6239-3

Printed and distributed by Amazon KDP.
www.kdp.amazon.com

Acknowledgements due to editors at *Dream Catcher Magazine*, in which 'The Girl I Ate Chinese In The Bath With, Isn't Who I Thought She Was', was featured in Issue 32 (Feb 2016), and published in *Wallflower* (Aug 2016).

Contact:
Twitter: /ashwatsonpoetry
Instagram: /ashwatsonpoetry

DEDICATED TO

Ash Kettle
My life.
And, the woman.
My woman.

WITH SPECIAL THANKS

to those in my life who never fail to inspire

Louisa Jackson
My best friend,
my firebringer,
my rock.

Lesley Burgin
The rhythm,
the wonder,
the warrior.

Sean Haughton
For support,
for reassurance,
for motivation.

CONTENTS

PART ONE

PART TWO

PART THREE

WOMAN

PART ONE

Some days
I am more wolf
than woman
and I am still learning
how to stop apologising
for my wild.

- Nikita Gill

Assumptions

They call me a *survivor*,
as if I sang a truth to be admired,
as if I just drift through wars.

They call me a *survivor*,
because the burns healed after the fire,
because I'm still capable of love.

They call me a *survivor*,
like it's something to be desired,
like I'm some kind of hero.

They call me a *survivor*,
with intentions to inspire me.
Without it, how would I cope?

They call me a *survivor*,
by assuming I've been broken.
So, could you fix me?

She-God

Do you know that she's a she-god?
Can't you tell by the way she
reaches beneath your skin,
pokes at the bone, exposed
from a selfish, previous love?
She likes to pluck at the chords
of your forgotten stitches at the root.
And if you knew she was a she-god,
you could have avoided this,
could have ripped away the petals
from the cherry blossom,
and fed on the centre,
spitting her out at the porch,
dabbing the corners of your mouth
with an old handkerchief,
doused in your mother's perfume.
She had passed it down from her mother,
and another mother before,
and it's threaded
like a lie tangled in the truth.
You've used it as a bookmark
until now, like it was stitched
to read into things.
Does she know that she's a she-god?
Yes, I think she does.

Making Love in a House of Mirrors

On the night you left me,
I began conversations with the moon.
I asked her what went wrong,
and she shrugged tired shoulders,

cursing and dancing the night away,
starry-skied and scarry-eyed,
tongue-tied by my bedside,
and she shrugged tired shoulders.

On the morning you came back,
I began slam poetry with the sun.
I asked her what went wrong,
and she shrugged tired shoulders,

shining her yellow love this way.
I notice the mirrors around the room,
and we could see our distorted selves,
appearing different in every reflection.

Every angle seemed so different,
every kiss, every freckle, every scar.
I asked you what went wrong,
and you shrugged naked shoulders.

I could see you, finally.

Avoiding the Lethal Drug That Is, Love

I wish I could be the frame
that surrounds your glass,
but I am nothing more than
the crack in the centre.
Pretty soon, I'll shatter,
and you'll either replace me,
or be exposed to the world
I find myself hiding away in,
leaving cracks in windows,
leaving gaps in shadows,
saying goodbye before
I cause any more destruction.
Because, darling,
the world is just too much
of a fragile place for me.

Embrace the Pain, in Fact, Buy It a Drink

We all slur love lyrics like bible quotes
at a stranger's funeral, letting the words
dance in the back of your mind, where
darkness resides between the spotlights.

In my dreams, we dress up the disasters
like the rain that pours after a storm,
washing away our being, completely,
and buying more drinks to pass the time.

Tomorrow we'll be rotten, forgotten-about,
scratchcards in the gutter, footprint-ridden,
worthless backends of a gambling urge.
I never was worth the risk, was I?

Even peeled back, revealing flesh,
all the fucks I had slowly drained away,
spreading themselves open into fog,
and shadows on the windowpane:

love hearts fingered on by inner child,
and initials breathing through our breath,
reminding us to embrace the pain,
and pour more drinks to pass the time.

Uptown Honey Lips

Your mascara eyes are
stained in the ceiling,
and they're still struggling
with your love.

Your work shoes have
gotten used to the feeling
of waiting by the door,
trying to be enough.

    You see,
you're an expert in seduction,
but an amateur in love.

Between pillow talk and
melting into the rug,
I breathe in the poison
from your lips.
Uptown Honey,
is the way it goes.

In town with
Uptown Honey Lips,
you show me the
best way to dance -
unstable tabletops
and tequila shots,
six more beers, and
the unveiling of soft spots.

Tell me,
how do your hands
cut like a knife?
Sharp beautiful blades,
trained to manipulate.

With every touch,
I could die
at the hands of
your uptown honey.

Evidently, Marie

I imagine you listening to the rain,
but never being caught in it.
I imagine you dressed in floral,
sangria on hand, Medi heat
absorbed by the light in your eyes.

I imagine it's obvious,
you taught her to be a woman.

I imagine hands held on the
darkest of nights and brightest of days.
I imagine harsh words exchanged from hurt,
the hurt being exchanged from love.

Yes, it's obvious,
you taught her to be a woman.

I imagine the way she looks at life,
is a reflection of you,
with some rebellion in her roots,
because you showed her to grow taller
and overlook the norms,
and embrace the rain in every storm.

It's obvious,
you taught her to be a woman.

I imagine Aaron Neville falling to pieces,
and white wine poured especially for you,

reading so deeply into things,
it strains your eyes, at times.

And sometimes,
she looks that way.

It's obvious,
you taught her to be a woman.

I imagine her love for purple
comes from you, lit up by the
dancing shadows of a million candles,
flames in sync with the fire of a
good memory she slowly dismantles,
brick by brick, her walls
come down around me.

It's obvious,
you taught her to be a woman.

I imagine the reason I am in awe
of your daughter, is because
you taught her to be a woman.

I Need a Cigarette Now

The smell of perfume in the shop,
on a business-as-usual Saturday night.
Mind's ticking, listening to heels clicking
on the tiled floor, I could just melt into.
Because now I'm thinking about you.

And I don't smoke,
but I need a cigarette now.

I need to revive my lungs
after seeing you again.

So I can't wait to turn off the open sign,
and find myself lost in the world tonight,
romanced by acoustics of police car hunger.
If I could plead insanity by love, I just might.
Because now I'm thinking about you.

And I don't smoke,
but I need a cigarette now.

Breathing is the only human thing
about me, and I've forgotten how.

The blankness in your eyes was like
a shotgun wound to the stomach.
I was blown away, by everything you had
to offer tonight, and everything you didn't.

And I don't smoke
but I need a cigarette now.

Hallucinations are clearer in the dark

and I'm tearing the walls down.

If I catch my breath,
I might say 'I love you'.

And I don't smoke
but I need a cigarette now.

You were my flame,
and I'm afraid to put the lighter down.

Quarantine

Give me the good wine,
the one where citrus bursts
in the back of our throats,
and burns a little,
considering the taste
before we swallow,
washing a worry away.

Pour it in the garden,
so the sun can shine
through the crystal,
into shadows on the wall
we drape ourselves over,
daring each other brick by brick.

And break up the fight
between this wasp and I.
We're having a staredown.
He's threatening to sting,
I'm threatening to sing.
Together we're tip-toeing
around the reality of everything.

Drink with me and eat it up, wasp.
You have nothing to complain about,
do you?

Isabelle's Door

The bill she couldn't pay was the final straw,
left her wandering into the dead of the night,
for shelter, light and warmth.

She sleeps in the doorway when it's wet,
curled up at the door, trying to ignore,
her hurt, anger and debt.

'Can you spare any?' she'd have said.
They shake their heads, with their pockets,
jangling each time they take a step.

Until the copper man stops, smiles,
paused and posed and poised, says
'Come with me, I'll make it worthwhile'.

She floats into the night, chest to air,
cleavage fashioned, temptress at work,
hair tangled, lipstick-smeared,

and back to the doorway,
body aching, shaking of bones,
dreaming of a better day.

Stardust Child

I was seven.
I saw a UFO.
I wished for it to take me away.

It's not that I wasn't happy.
I didn't *not* like my life.
I just wanted more.

I was seven,
and already getting bored.

I was seven.
I enjoyed walks in the rain,
watching it come down hard,
the world rushing away inside,
becoming absorbed
in street-like graveyards.

I was seven.
This was always the good part.
I knew the true meaning
of 'ghost', 'aching hearts',
and 'art overdose'.

I was seven,
wanting more from my radio.

I was seven,
just waiting for the UFO.

Twenty-Something Cans of Monster Energy

The essence of adolescence
is the twenty-something
cans of Monster Energy,
wedged beneath the hedge

behind the rec, wrecked,
grass up to its neck in
Mars Bar wrappers
they left for dead.

They're tip-toeing. Treading,
on ice so thin that parents
are being called in to
explain broken cider bottles

and why their kid's life
is a mess. And why
their life is on a cliffside,
dancing on the edge.

The essence of adolescence
is the tattoo of black marker pen -
kids waiting for it to get dark and then,
scrawling each other's names on
lonely-looking street signs just to feel like
a permanent part of the world again.

Dear Chloe Who-Graffitied-Her-Name
On-Douglas-Avenue-Street-Sign,

I hope the taste of the ink has
left you satisfied. Dignified. Justified.
Kept your mind occupied...

or just happier than you originally realised.

I'll think of you tonight,
if I dare to close my eyes.

Limbo

You shattered me into pieces
and watched me crumble between us.

You saw me descend into the earth,
and walked back out of my world.

You swept me under the rug,
and left me there to live.

Your kiss is something else entirely.
It still creates a fire inside of me.

You are the love of my life,
and the deadliest weapon.

Trapped in a purgatory of love,
I am forever a ghost, in limbo.

Aching in places I didn't know I had,
I'm climbing the walls with my sanity,

drinking until my liver bleeds
smoking until my lungs blacken.

Self-destruction is familiar now,
and it's somewhat comforting.

The Interview

So you're dating.
Tasting wine in foreign restaurants,
linking hands beside the candle's burn,
talking about...

you.
Like some kind of interview.

You're smiling to ease the fake formality,
laughing at his jokes,
easing into a goodnight kiss to say,

    yes,

you've fallen in love.

Kingdom

I looked into your eyes
as you bled into mine,
and you said...
do you see the damage?

And all of a sudden,
your lips could build a castle,
as powerful as your history.

You kissed me so hard,
tears fought their way out
like a daydream with an agenda.

So yes,
I could see the damage.

And I could taste it,
washing over your kiss
like a storm was passing.

I know now, it was a goodbye.
I was never meant to be
a part of your kingdom.

Dance Floor Silhouette

The music binds to your bones,
via vibrations through toes
to fingertips,
swinging through the smoke.

The lights from the stage,
paint shadows of your name,
and a silhouette,
swaying in the rain.

The excitement in your eyes,
brings me back to life.
I am a dancing corpse,
falling in the night.

And I'm no good for you,
because I bring out the best in you.
You crave a fuck-up
who doesn't see you.

I see the damsel in distress,
dressed up in your flaws.
I am a dance floor silhouette,
and you are the cause.

Reassuring Our Death

Surely, if you are the first thing I think of
before my eyes close for the night,
only to open again, and be reborn
with thoughts of you,

then surely,
        you are my fire and my magic.

And if you are the only thing
I think of when my eyes finally close,
and with each blink, each breath,
I hear the lies of our love,
I'll see the death.

So surely,
        she was your fire, and your magic.

Love, you've ruined me.
I've never been so sure.

Skeleton in My Bathroom

As I shower,
water masks my eyes,
and she stands in the corner
of my mind, lurking.

And the steam
is choking her,
like excessive words,
like tongue twisters,
and she doesn't know
what they mean.

While her memories
try to muffle her screams,
she eyes up her scars,
and nobody knows
what they've seen.

She was riding life,
being told that anxiety
is nothing more than
a state of our living,
and the way we think
is a result of our inner feelings.

Trapped,
like a skeleton
in my bathroom.
But she's choking

on the steam,
she's fingering messages
on the window,
for the nurse,
telling her to

calm
     the
          fuck
               down.

Kate

What if you fall in love?
Then what would I do?
I wouldn't be able to stand it.
And it's selfish, I know.
I'm an asshole, I know.
I wouldn't be able to stand it.

It would be like losing a bet,
where you've gambled away
every part of yourself.
All the cards are on the table,
and you never learned how to bluff.
And there's a hunger to feed,
because it hurts more
to let her starve.

What if you fall in love?
Then what would I say?
I'd bite my tongue until I bleed,
and savour the taste.

Every part of me is now on the table.
There's nothing else to offer.
There's nothing else to say.

And this hunger continues to drink,
because it hurts more
to let her starve.

If I cut myself open,
would you still fall in love?
If you were inked across my chest,
would you be able to stand me?

My Friend Doesn't Drink

and so how am I supposed
to keep in tune with her sanity?
Or the way she talks mundanities
as I ponder cause and effect of wine
in my previous dancefloor tragedies?

She watches the world rotate,
similar to the way my head spins.
Yet I somehow manage
to build a house of beer mats
out of what might-have-beens.

And her hips sway to the bar,
swimming to the rhythm
of drums and an electric guitar,
images sticking to my memory
like the spilt ale on my arms.

And she knows all of the words,
slamming *Summer of '69*
and doing a bloody fine job.
I got my first real six-string...
and a shot. And a shot. A shot.

Seduction Weapon

Her hand fists around her
seduction weapon
to hold her body up
with her curves romancing,
the men who don't see
the weakness in her knees
or her sweat and aching
from all the dancing.

Or her burning stench
of dirty cologne, on her
naked arms, just skin and bones
shaking like they're about to snap,
her body's about to collapse
but she doesn't sit to breathe.

No, she sits on strangers' laps,
kissing at necks as they plant
a ten down the front of her pants.
And this is so her daughter,
at the age of five, can have a roof
over her head, as she closes her eyes.

I never wanted this kind of life.

He is the reason
she talks in her sleep,
dances weekend nights

feeling tired and cheap.
All because he made a
promise he couldn't keep.
One night of 'short and sweet' love,
was more than he could possibly need.

And so her hand fists around her
seduction weapon,
her curves romancing the men;
her body dancing again.

Screwed-Up Society

Three a.m. and hot.
My palms were sweating anyway.
What is it with hormone-raging
teens, and the urge to gather
in the night?

"Kiss me," she whispered.

I could smell her breath,
lingering on my cheeks.
My knees, weak, trying
to steady my shaking body.
My sweaty palms now
clinging to blades of grass,
poking through my fingers.

The taste of her lips...
like little cherry daggers,
stabbing into me.

I wanted to jump in the lake.

I wanted to sink, not drown,
and then float again.
I wanted to hide from
a beautiful reality of
being infatuated with the girl.

I never wanted to be a wallflower;
I sat beside my desperate need
to peel myself off and spread
out my leaves and grow.

Now, I will quite happily
shrivel up in the corner with you,
tangled in your branches because
that's what I was made to do.

What would've happened if I
ignored my response to you,
and went about my life the way
they say you're 'supposed to'?

I would want to jump in the lake.

I would be floating in the water,
allowing my soul to dance around
those who actually want to see it.

"Kiss me,"
And I did.

But I wanted to jump in the lake.

Tattoo

With the tips
of my fingers,
I want to trace
every line
of ink
on your body –
to feel the pain
you went through
to express your art,
the permanence
of your love
for it,
and the way
it looks so great
on your
skin.

Bristles

You've gotten into my bones.
It makes me want to snap,
everything I have.

Makes me want to snap into a woman,
breathing fire at the thought of our existence.
My body, your body, breathing fire.

We could tame the flames with our mouths,
blowing away the smoke, if we would dare to.
Or admire one another's burns.

And if we turn to ashes,
I'll sweep you up with the bristles
nobody else can see.

Wine

I'm sorry
that I let you slip
through my fingers
and fall,
watch you
disappear
into a
never-ending
journey.
Or so it seemed.
I'm sorry that
the outcome
was a hundred
tiny pieces of
smashed glass.
And I'm sorry
I didn't
bleed
when I picked
you up.
But I'm glad
you were empty.
You would have
stained.

A Ghost of You

How could I explain my situation?
Or the way it bruises my mind
over and over and over again?

Well, I suppose the thought of reviving you
involves the killing of things I love about me,
to only be reunited with a ghost of you.

And I have already witnessed and seen
clearly through your transparency,
both your falseness and weaknesses.

That's why I'm spooked.
I'm forever haunted by both
your absence and your presence.

Yet we swallow the same taste life has to offer.
we practically breathe one another's words,
while I am grieving for you, and feeling so lost

in a crowd with no way out.
But then there are days I'd rather be lost,
completely surrounded by picture-frames,

where things are so less complicated.
So how do I explain my situation,
if I don't even understand it myself?

Fences

She cuts her arms
the way she plays violin,
and through her eyes,
her mind wanders
like a bird in the winter.
None of us know, really,
where they go.

Over fences, behind the trees,
through the clouds, and
back into the rose bush.

We're feeling more like dandelions,
clawing back at the earth.
Our yellow fangs can really bite.

Maybe there is music
in the way we bleed.
Maybe you needed to hear it.
Maybe you liked the sound, of
splitting yourself open like rose on thorn,
or shadows on the fences.

I can't tell you not to wander.
But I won't sleep tonight,
if I don't ask you not to.

PART TWO

At twenty I tried to die
And get back, back, back to you.
I thought even the bones would do.

- Sylvia Plath

Abstract

I'm thinking about she,
whose mouth draped in the dark
over collarbone, making shapes
with wet kiss and fluttering form.

I wonder, was she trying to start
a war between tongue and gums,
or making way for the teeth?

Were hands always stitched this way,
moulding and squirming and
transforming the heat into love?

Were they built to finger at her
dimples or glass jaw bone,
scratching into melted form?

She would fixate on black and white
photographs, like conspiracies
scooping her up and dropping her
into the water to sink, like a
wedding ring in a bubble bath.

And she would be fascinated by
the colour of the soap, catching on the
spike of her brows beneath the surface,
combing at me to pull her out, or jump in
and submerge my own fins.

I would always choose the latter,
partying in the ruffles and waves,
dancing with octopus emotions
drenched in vinegar and salt.

I like to think some hero would find us
here among the dead, and he might
notice the dangers of falling inside our
own minds the way we already have.

He may see the way we hold each other,
like sand moving through an hourglass:
complete weightlessness
and blurred-out boundaries.

And he would go home to his love, wrestle
his arm around her waist like a stomach knot
that doesn't unravel, and she would demand
he holds her at the hips as she hovers.

Just like that, we latched onto vines again,
trying to lift us out from swimming lights
we felt so mesmerised by, and fixate on the
bedroom walls instead, showered in
forget-me-nots and shadows from the
wardrobe door that wouldn't shut.

And her thumbs press into my cheeks,
and she screams into my mouth:
why do you love me?

Dressed Down

I want to see the woman dressed down.
The woman who makes dressing gowns
sexy, almost better on, than off.
There's something about the silk.

I want to see the woman dressed down,
removing her party wear for slippers,
crap films and Sunday morning kisses,
and everything my heart has been missing.

I want to see the woman dressed down,
when her hair isn't perfect, when it's
messy like our minds, when her eyes,
untouched, have nothing to fear but mine.

I want to see the woman dressed down,
wearing nothing but a smile, and my hands,
wandering miles, between naked sheets
and your 'I don't give a fuck' style.

I want to see the woman dressed down,
whiskey sours downed in the living room,
lights off, dancing to her favourite song,
with a lost sense of right and wrong tonight.

I want to see the woman dressed down,
from curled lashes to ankle tattoos,
birthmarks, wrinkles and scars,
and everything the world never knew.

I want to see the woman dressed down,
because I need to know if it's love.

The Girl I Ate Chinese in the Bath With Isn't, Who I Thought She Was

Brunette I used to see.
Still see.
Hair drooping over
her shoulders like
wet curtains of seduction,
drying at the tips
and at the fringe,
brushed back behind
those ears I loved to kiss.
Would love to kiss.
I'm still completely
submerged
in her. Her legs
dangling over
the edge like towels
hanging out to dry,
her wrinkly fingertips
linked in mine,
the sweetness of
wine on her breath,
and the taste of it
leaving my head
an irreversible mess.
She was chaotic,
and this is not a love poem.

Beautiful Things

For Louisa

Maybe I'm imagining things now,
but I feel as though I see you, now.
You're listening to Morrissey,
one hand piecing together shards
of your soul, the other holding a gin.
And the combination works beautifully.

You see, I too know all the words to
Everyday Is Like Sunday
but you do it more justice than me.

I can tell you're a beautiful person
just by the way you clap to *Radio Gaga*,
dig deep into the things you love,
stand proud by the people you love,
laugh at ridiculous things that
never do seem ridiculous anymore.

And you wear that delicate heart of yours,
like a beautiful stain on your sleeve -
proud to be you but sleepwalking through life,
searching for things to believe in.

Beautiful things.

Like unbeatable background noise or
damaged words from a beautiful voice or

an alternate reality, or good wine, or
lounging in the garden on summer nights,
or maybe the way you always hug goodbye.

Every little thing is a beautiful thing.

Empty Avenues

Cigarettes rested between fingers,
fingers rested on grains of sugar,
but life wasn't always too sweet
from the view of the fruit bowl.

Rotten bananas looked lonely in
the moonlight, tea droplets would
melt to sad faces in the marble.
Even teaspoons can't let go.

At three a.m. she takes to the curtains,
fascinated by ghost town attire,
and getting lost there for a moment,
flirting with the idea of walking away.

But destinations are never certain
and bedroom windows are beautiful.
Our eyes could run for miles
and never be ready for the travel.

So her smile is the invisible footsteps
and lamplight of other houses tonight.
I wish her the sweetest of dreams,
from silent screams of empty avenues.

Midnight Drive

We trash-talked
over sambuca shots in the dark,
then wrote poetry
on the back seat of the car.

Your fingernails glistened
through raindrops on the window,
with your fists clenched
over the wheel, rearing to go.

We said we'd drive to a town
that nobody knows.
But like your feet,
your hands were so cold.

We could go,
             you said.

We could disappear like
smashed windows, cracking a smile.
The colours on the walls
would wave us goodbye.
Gutters would sing lullabies
like it's their last song.
And we could be happy,
you and me.

We said we'd drive to a town
that nobody knows.

But like our minds,
your heart was growing old.

We could stay,
                    you said.

You never could make up your mind.

Stilettos and Capes

On a typical Saturday night, your eyes
would hypnotise me beyond the stairs.

But tonight I'm aware of everything,
and the light in your eyes changed
through the bottom of my drink.

I'll avoid these dangers within us,
the hunky-dory sense of calm
before the storm, this anxiety-ridden
dance of love and hate, skipping
along the edge of cliffsides, wearing
your favourite stilettos and a cape.

I would call you my pretty little bird,
with a choice of staying, falling, or flying,
depending on the colour of your mood.

Last Saturday night, I could make you move,
away from the edge for a better view.

But this Saturday night, you had
enough fire to burn me inside out,
unloading our passion with the heat.
But you put out the flames
when you left me in the sheets.

And like a typical Sunday morning,
I cling to the edge of the cliffside,

praying I'll see you again today,
hoping you'll dance with me that way,
in stilettos and a cape.

Femme Fatale

She makes me want to dissect the sun
to see why it shines for her.

She tells me to dig up the earth,
to see what I'm made of.

She lets me run between flames,
knowing I'll be scarred forever.

She pulls me out of the flames,
and whispers 'we can be heroes'.

She looks at me like I can change the world,
but my universe has never been smaller.

She kisses me like there's no tomorrow,
but still, I fall asleep so easily.

And I dream of my dollhouse state,
my body, moving like a wave.

And she floats away with me,
on the surface of false perfections,

melting into the burning of this sun,
she pulls apart everything I have.

But still, I fall asleep so easily.
She breaks me, so beautifully.

Cherry Goddess

I would compare your skin to a
healthy tobacco smoke, diving
through your clouds, and into the
bowl of cherries on your stomach.

I would breathe you in, just like
a smoker would, and could,
topping up your womanhood
with a glass of whiskey and love.

And you would challenge me,
to a cherry knot competition,
to see whose kiss is superior,
and then test out the theory.

We could have stayed out there
forever, growing out our grass limbs
from muddy hearts and dust,
slowly getting back to our roots.

But there was a life to return to,
somewhere in the summer,
where the sun hadn't shaded
your ink. Not quite just yet.

And you hadn't rescued a June bug,
because they have it all figured out.
And the last chapter of the book
you were reading never ended.

And if the world stops turning again,
maybe we can revisit ourselves here.
I would challenge you to a rematch,
calling dibs on the cherry bowl.

Mona Lisa Mind

Your heart is stained on your shirt
with scars like caged introverts.
Please, don't walk away
from this world.

You're blessed with a
Mona Lisa mind
and by this, I mean
it's a fucking masterpiece.

There is art between us,
between the sheets,
colours in every breath,
painting every heartbeat.
But in your kiss is where
I found the poetry.

I know you get lost at
your window in the night
but you won't find love
in the shadow of a streetlight.
Let me in and we can search
the corners of your mind.

That shirt you're wearing
is my favourite,
and you've paid for it
by looking so good in it.
It brings out the heart

on your sleeve,
still wearing it out
as your slide your coat
on top
       and leave.

How the hell am I
supposed to sleep,
with only a slight chance
I'll see you in my dreams?

Mona Lisa mind
just met The Scream.
I am a ghost on the boardwalk,
hiding from the sea.

Kiss me like you never
want to be lonely again.
We can walk away
from this world together.

Your Favourite Tattoo

I'm in love with
your favourite tattoo
because you showed me
your favourite tattoo
and told me the story behind
your favourite tattoo.
I'm in love with
your favourite tattoo.

And there's just
something about the ink,
a faded sort of sexy mistake
you don't regret.
But I suppose that's the story
of a favourite tattoo.
Good scars, and bad times,
and your 'can do' attitude.

I'm in love with
the layers of art,
as you undress, your
designs tear me apart.
But before you switch out
the light tonight,
you should show me
your second favourite tattoo.

Fragments of a Romance

Pulled out of bed
by the thought of you,
pulled into bed
by the sight of you.

Pulled out of every
comfort zone I come across
for a breath, making mistakes
and promises to be made.

Pulled into your arms,
pushed away again,
drawn in by your perfume,
released from the sting,

I am tied up by the
softness of your hands,
pulling me everywhere
they're wandering.

Storm brewing, raindrops
pulling me to the window.
Shoulder. Hands. Cup of tea.
Back to bed.

My mind likes to spin
when you start singing,
my eyes are absorbed
in your dancing,

and then you romance
the fuck out of me.

Your dress lies lifeless
on the bedroom floor,
with my shell of a
leather jacket and 3000 kisses,

and every time your eyes
flutter as you sleep
I am pulled back into a reality
I can't keep up with.

Storm brewing, raindrops
pulling me to the window.
Fragments of a romance
stitching me away.

Drum Solo

We were in that space,
where the world had stopped
and it was just our hands
wandering,
as we listened to music
that never stopped or faded out.

It was a bottle of wine, and Phil Collins,
and kissing, and waiting for the drum solo.
It was the way you fell back on the sofa,
spelling out:

"I want you, *now*."
    "I want you, *here*."
        "I want you to want me, now."
                "I want you to want me, here."

I spelled out an 'okay' with the way I held you.

We were in that space,
where the world has stopped,
and it was just my hands,
wrapped around you,
as we listened to music
that eventually

        f a d e d   o u t.

There's Something Sexy About Thighs

I have a thing about thighs.
They catch my eye as you walk by,
and I strike up conversation as a disguise,
while in my mind, I start to fantasise.

Not like that.

I just think you're beautiful.
You're a pleasant surprise,
like a downpour of rain in July
or a sunrise over an evening sky.

I know I sound like a cliché,
and a complete ass right now,
but it's these that come to mind.
Basically, I can't keep my eyes

off of you. And, woman, I need to.
My head is spinning anti-clockwise
planning sexy rendezvous'.
So, walk over here, won't you?

Mrs extra skin-tight skinny jeans
in a preferred risqué black, not blue.
Put me out of my misery, won't you?
If I asked you for a drink tonight,

you'd say no, wouldn't you?

Maybe I make you nervous
with the way I fixate on things.
But I am just a passionate person.

So Miss-I-could-call-you-sexy-thighs-
but-instead-call-you-miss-beautiful-mind,
make a bed by my side and lie,
as if the stars have been perfectly aligned.

We can be the stars of our own show.
No audience. Just a spotlight and us,
dancing to music only we can hear,
where sexy thighs do all the talking.

Stories Through Wine Bottles

Tasting a 'trust me' kiss, as you hold my
Heart in your coat pocket for safe-keeping.
Inside your mind is a fucking wonderland,
Speaking music until it makes me dance.

I have never been in the mood for endless
Soul-searching on sleepless nights, but
Nights are for soul-searching, right?
Through to morning, I still question my life.

Everything about you is beautiful.
Veins are split open to reveal the truth.
Everyone is bleeding behind the bulletproof,
Raining like the world collapsed on the roof.
You're not safe in a house of brokenness but
That is a story to tell through wine bottles.
Hell is a myth that is likely to exist, so
Ignite fire with the flames of your hands, and
Never stop the burning of your
Green eyes.

Yesterday's news is not something I live by.
Over-dramatised lust is not my type but
Under-the-weather with love just might be.

And inside your mind is a fucking wonderland.
Reckless, chaotic, and beautifully damned.
Everything you touch is a fucking wonderland.

Route of Desire

Your kisses come in slick,
buttering me up through the streets
of my body.

There are lanes and lanes of me,
falling asleep like abandoned trolleys
in jitties left to rust, sinking

in potholes of 'pay and display' car parks,
and streetlights that haven't worked
since 2015,

forgotten about on these dead-end roads,
still playing saxophone through our stomachs
pressed together in stalls.

We were drunk on the idea, of forgetting
hot nights on the town that would detach us
from all we know.

So we forced our eyes shut for a moment,
encasing our neck bones with our hands,
and put up more roadblocks.

Denim Dreams

I love how you cling
onto my jacket and kiss;
fists clenched, fingers
twisted round sleeves,
knuckles love-punching
into denim dreams.

When did I spill a pint
of lager down my jeans?
Was it before or after
I stumbled down the street
in hopes for an early night,
without coming close to sleep?

Instead, I built some walls
out of poetry books,
wondering about these poets
and what it all means.
It was the perfect end to a
weekend night for me.

And as I wandered
home alone in the dark
I also wonder about this
scavenger hunt for your heart,
searching for all the
meanings behind the art.

But I still love how you kiss,

clinging to me with fists
around the sleeves,
your fingers dance and twist,
knuckles love-punching
into denim dreams.

Love Is Fire

I hid tulips under all the pillows,
then set fire to the house.
In the flames was every letter you wrote,
every picture of us burning to ash,
lipstick melting into the floorboards,
like it would in Morocco, only
the smoke smells better than summer.

I no longer breathe in your nightmares
or choke on the lies you told.
My lungs have never been so clear.

And Bukowski once said:

*"what matters most is
how well you walk through the fire."*

But I'm running through flames,
with everything I have, trying
to get to you and get away from you.
My lungs have never been so confused.

My lungs would rather burn
without you.

Storm of a Thought

You are this beautifully broken thing,
that I can never fix.

There's poison in your kiss,
because I am sucked into the abyss.

This,
    it's a storm of a thought,

of never being good enough,
and wanting to be good enough for you.

of wanting to create distance
but feeling my lungs twisting,
as I simply can't breathe without you.

of questioning every word falling from
that beautiful mouth of yours.

You've got me reading between every
word now, because it might mean more.
It's one of my many, many flaws.

I try to find excuses at the
bottom of a bottle,

digging up exchanges that should
have been forgotten,

But you're a drug.
    My mind is an addict
        And my body is rotting
                from the inside out.

I've never told you that
I'm scared to touch you,
but it's the undeniable truth.

I'm terrified of you,
either breaking in my hands,
or falling to your feet in front of you.
Because I would just fall to hell with you.

You have complete control over me.
That is a beautifully scary thought.

And I think I am in love with you.
And this deadly storm of a thought.

Perfume and Flashbacks

I walk past the perfume shop
inhaling flashbacks of you.

My palms began to sweat.
They always used to.

My mouth dried up.
It always would do.

I walk into the perfume shop,
finding myself smiling,

as my heart began to race
at the thought of

my lips on your lips,
savouring your taste.

"Excuse me," she says.
"Could I squeeze past?"

"Sorry," I say,
as I buy the perfume.

Enough to Die

Darling, you continue to surprise,
burying everything deep enough to die.
I can see the love tearing from your eyes.

And I could drown in a sunset sky,
gasp for breath long enough to die.
Darling, you continue to surprise.

I think I may completely lose my mind,
trying to find my way back home tonight,
after seeing the love tearing from your eyes.

Life scares you so much you've tried to hide,
speaking a thousand words with a single lie.
Darling, you continue to surprise,
I can see the love tearing from your eyes.

Sweet Beat Poetry

She wandered
down the street
like a kind of
street poetry;
like a kind of
sweet beat poetry.

And I went full-on
poet mode.

You could tell
by my hands,
itching for a pen
to download words,
from mind to page
as they jumbled
in my head
and my body
began to overload.

Sweet beat poetry.

And I sewed a story
between thumb and finger,
before it could
escape through
my throat, or choke.

Then she stopped

at the traffic lights.
Cars began to slow.

Stop. Please, stop.

She walked on.
Traffic continued to flow,
and I'm left with a
sweet beat poem.

And nobody
will ever know.

If You Was a Villanelle

You complicate things with your eyes.
They tell me stories, dancing with mine.
And complication is a beautiful disguise.

Darling, I hate that you tip-toe through life,
afraid of dressing up your heart tonight.
God, you complicate things with your eyes.

You're like a song I haven't heard in ages,
complicating with your lips tonight, and mine.
And complication is a beautiful disguise.

And why are you looking at me like that?
I'm trying to read the poetry from your mind
but you just complicate things with your eyes.

You don't sing as loud as you used to,
and we're hiding from the world tonight.
Complication is a beautiful disguise.

And you have the most beautiful mind,
it's my favourite escape from time to time.
You complicate things with your eyes,
and complication is a beautiful disguise.

We Are Strangers Inside These Walls

You're fixated
on everything
but me

and I'm fixated
on you,

wondering if
you'll ever fixate
on me.

We are strangers
inside these walls,
and I feel like
making them fall,

if they could ever
fall for me.
It would be hard
to fall for *me*.

And I will never
be the art,

I am brick, with
a concrete heart.

I am a ghost
with beautiful scars.

You are Sunday morning
music, that has never
seen the dark.

And you fixate
on everything
but me.

Writing a Tragedy

Remember I am a
           creative destruction,

and you are
           tragedy-meets-seduction.

You are beautiful
in the way we see
fireflies dancing around
a black sky,

fading into the night
           with perfection.

My love, you are
something else entirely,
staining my mind
with that face of yours.

I'm dizzy now,
from head vs heart wars.
And I don't think I care anymore.
I know what I want now.

But I rip my insides out
and put it on paper.
Words are friends but
emotions are strangers.

I could destroy it all
with my love for you.
Because that's always
been easier to do.

And I never do
take the easier route.

I am this
creative destruction,

and you, a
tragedy-meets-seduction.

I am starving for you,
and I am writing to you,
in a never-ending cycle
of resurrection –

a never-ending cycle
of screwed-up perfection.

Lake Louise

If my skin could
soak up the water,
I would wash away
everything,
and float forever,

getting lost in this
blue world -
burning through
the ice
with the thought
of your touch,
drowning in this life
with the thought
of your love.

Darling, is paradise
enough for you
if the mountains
should hide us here?
Now, we'll never
truly go home.

My heart is still
swimming between
rocky mountains,
under close-watch
of bears and elk,
and in the eyes of you.

And it's hard to say
which is most beautiful,
because everything
feels right here,
at Lake Louise,
with you near.

Hotel Room in London

The sound of the river
beneath my window,
drowns out the noise of
this deafening silence.

But the sheets don't
smell of you.
It can't fix that.

And I started to think
the river can't fix much.
It can't fix a broken watch
or shirts we threw into the fire.

It can't fix a sleeping pattern
sleepwalking through the day.
It can't fix the way music
breaks my heart and
soothes my bones.

It can't fix the
sickness of wine in my mouth,
the morning after the shout.

It can't fix an open wound
no matter what caused it.

It can't fix my hatred for mirrors,
or my love for darkness,

or your fear of darkness,
or the way you tremble here somehow.

The sheets don't smell of you,
and I want to burn them alive
and descend to the river.

PART THREE

'Cause I'm a woman
Phenomenally.
Phenomenal woman,
That's me.

– Maya Angelou

Beer Kisses

I'm reading into a woman
who crafts true living in the
centre of the palm of her hands,
and the way she forms a
whirlwind of disaster within me.
At the moment she is surrounded,
consumed by beer bottles ganging
up for a swag of her ballerina untouch.
We know that true talent lies within
the alien breeze of her kiss, blowing
bubbles into the sky as if they're
a force to be reckoned with,
as if cherry aroma could be any
crueller than salmon fingertips,
tea rose nails tracing ink on bare skin.
Behind glass, I watch her knuckles
light fires, moving like a butterfly
dancing on the sea. Tell me,
what does it mean to drown?
You said the sky looks better
from beneath the surface, dripping
with a premature envy in this museum
of lungs, breathing in memories
of shoelace-ravelled finger bones.
She thinks about her mother, the dress
she wore on her wedding night,
sizzled in moonlight heat like a
cocktail of petrol and flame, laughing
at the way she can burn so brightly.

She says "help me
bring this dark landscape to life"
It makes me think of my love.
We began our journey, through
crawling on our knees and crying
in our hands, getting lost in the
reality of everything we're scared to be:
maze runners on the straight and narrow.
Near the end of the road, we
couldn't believe how far we had come,
with tired wings flying and dying,
and flying and dying, and wilting
and waiting, and flying again.
And flying; we were always flying.

Queen of Melodrama

I could hear you through the wall,
smashing every plate in the kitchen.
Even your favourite was in the etchings,
and soon to be swept away.

I called you the Queen of Melodrama,
because it was easier that way,
easier than accepting that need,
to sweep it all away again.

In the morning we used the old bowls,
scratched and chipped and delicate,
like many of us, I'd say, lately.
And we chewed away silently.

By lunchtime, sad Sunday songs
played on the radio with bad signal,
but in their own time, began slow-
dancing through the hallway with me.

And in the evening, we spun
teacups on sharded glass tumblers.
I was at ease when the darkness,
could simply sweep me away.

Morning Routine

In the mornings, I scrunch at my hair,
and my fingers tangle between the knots.
And as I tug, I calmly assure myself:
You've got some work to do.

I pull my eyelids down, over my cheeks,
and for a moment, the circles disappear.
It's an attempt to keep my eyes open.
They could close forever.

The water stings at first, like all new starts do.
The cold shoots through every nerve.
Then, the worries rinse and drain away,
as I spit out the bad taste of yesterday.

I lay out the law with my reflection,
and I notice the cracks in the mirror,
gambling between specks of toothpaste.
I wonder, how haven't I noticed these before?

The cracks line up as scars on her skin,
as she dances with the wolves within.
She welcomes the day, but won't ever face it.
This lifeless soul is completely misplaced here.

I pull my eyelids down, over my cheeks,
and for a moment, my world disappears.

Forest

Me and this dead oak tree,
have come to an understanding.
Today, she visits me in my sleep,
and I worship her rotted roots,
knees submerged in the dirt where
her twisted limbs are buried.
She's still singing down there,
listening to me digging away,
separating shards of loose bark,
crunching old rimpled leaves,
scattered like black pepper grains
on raw and bleeding steak cuts,
melt-in-the-mouth distaste,
teeth marks of the earth.
Tomorrow, she reaches her
branches into me, blossoming
through my punctured soul,
and lifts me out of this forest.

Photograph of My Mother in Her Thirty-Third Year

after Raymond Carver

You hate photos of yourself.
You analyse every angle of your curves,
every crease, wrinkle, bump, needing a
closer look, at such shitty observations.
I've never understood, what it is you see.

One particular picture comes to mind,
taken from your thirty-third year,
and also your wedding day.

In case Dad never noticed, the camera flash
caught every shade of hazel in your eyes,
and darkened out the world behind you.

They became shadows in the ashes, with just
features of a lit cigarette, and a genuine smile.
And before it crosses your mind - no.

No love-handles or crows-feet in sight,
because you were thirty-three, Mum.
You have yet to spend another twenty years
watching me grow into a woman,

witness my first failures and successes,
discover my passions and ambitions,
see me fall in love for the first time,

or simple things, like telling you time and time
again, that yes, I drink my coffee black,
and no, I don't take sugar.

Your butterfly brain refuses to settle,
beautiful, delicate, and designed to fly,
with blinding colours and an intense mind.

And still, you hate photos of yourself,
and me, I've never understood why.

Moongazer

His beat fedora has hopes of better days,
grey upon grey, and grey upon silver,
and chapped lips, and battered zips,
working man's hands and wife's last kiss.

His jacket is torn, the way heartstrings
can pull at sadness and rip into love,
because what he has could be enough.
He's angry with his hit and miss life,

cursed by fading memories
between haunted childhood streets
to wandering the house at 4am,
still drinking her favourite wine.

On her side of the bed, he wraps
tired fingertips to shoulder blades
with a need to feel something, anything,
raising a glass to someone, anyone.

Her perfume that would choke him,
does well to linger here too.
At 5am, things change again.
The sun appears, and outside the world

moves on effortlessly, like it could be
sucked through a straw and spat back out.
We do this every day, don't we?
We're angry with and without a pot to piss in,

desperately taming anarchy within ourselves,
burying the dead if we should find them there,
and whispering, "we want no trouble here."
The trouble is already out there.

Oregano

My hands look older,
scarred for decoration,
pink discolouration,
and blue thread
knitting me together.

They heal slower,
and nails break,
knuckles clicking into
routines and snapping,
to cushion the cradling
of Pinot Grigio.

Fingertips season
oregano to precision,
but bruise after hand-holding,
and ache at the lack of it.
So is this love?

Offers on moisturiser
suddenly appeal,
and the smell of it
soothes sliced grooves
on finger joints,
grappling yesterday's stitch.

Drying out, like the old shirt
from a memory,
wrinkles are embraced

and absorbed,
back into existence
and back out of
decoration.

The Rhythm

for Lesley

Your sense of humour
is like a dance through the city
with every disco light shining for you.

And everyone hits the floor, perfectly.
It seems that we all have a rhythm.
You show me the way we move.

And you,
you know how to laugh.
Really, laugh.

At yourself, and me,
through visions only you see,
in which these scenarios play out.

And god,
you know how to laugh.
Truly, laugh.

Your love for the simple things,
is the most complex thing
anyone could have.

Even the cruellest curveballs
keep your spirits high,

and so, to me,
you are a dance through the city,
keeping the lights alive.

Undiscovered

Opposite Shipley tea rooms,
hay bales roll into summer,

the way we roll into each other,
and we would try to jump them

like teenagers in cliché horrors,
prizing fingers into the golden tails

for a grip, and falling backwards
into bottomless pits of youth,

convinced and compelled
in dying sunlight, this will last.

And she, between checkered
flannel shirt, black nail paint

and thespian eyeliner art,
flares into leaf and bone,

on woodland theatre stage,
and leads me into the show,

with backdrops of pink sky,
blue jeans on golden straw bench,

and undiscovered colours,
blending into blank canvases.

Love Was...

stumbling around in the dark,
trying to find the light switch.

It was carpet burns on naked skin.
It was all the broken promises
and the secrets in between.

Love was running to you
in the middle of the night,
and running ever since.

It was the candle flickers in the
reflection of your eyes, and yes,
it was your dress last Friday night.

It was Stevie Nicks on the radio,
a bottle of wine and one glass,
a bottle of wine and two glasses.

Love was sleepwalking away
from the pain of warm bed sheets,
cold bedsheets, and the thought
of another love scene.

It was in the electricity of your kiss.
It was your favourite lipstick on your
favourite coffee mug, and love was,
envying the same coffee mug.

It was your favourite line of poetry,
and the way you spoke your
favourite line of poetry.
Love was in all the lines of poetry.

It was your love of candles,
songs from years ago.
It was the lamplight instead of chandeliers
and sweeping your hair behind your ears.

Love is torn-up pieces inside of me.
Love is everything I wanted us to be.
And I'm still crawling around in the dark,
trying to find the light switch.

Some Things Never Change

I aged as I kissed her.

Her eyes aged fifty,
hips aged twenty,
lip work like a teen.

She's had a difficult life
with a wonderful mind.

And I challenge her,
through chapters of her life,

daring her.

The outcome
is always the same.

The Woman on the Bus to Nowhere

She doesn't want to ride the bus today.
She wants to fall into the melting concrete,
drown in it, be part of it, roast under the sun
like winter burns into summer, and live in it.

She wants to see a world where a man
might only love for the eyes, and she
wouldn't blank the truth or savour the lies.
And she doesn't know me at all.

I see her eyes in the bottom of a wine glass,
and as the last sip kicks, it pulls us in like
a kiss on a mind trip, and I hang on
every word falling from her lips.

I watch her scan love interests
as they pass her by, shifting loosely
in her seat, so she can analyse.
I watch a tireless mind through
storytelling eyes, searching for perfection
that doesn't exist in the light.

And I catch those eyes, hypnotised,
but I don't think she read me right.
I am not worthy of a second beautiful look.
I was written out of her mental rule book of

people I could fall in love with,
or out of bed with.

And I could talk for hours, digging around
in the closet of our fucked up minds.
I want to know everything that makes her tick,
everything that moves her, consumes her.

And she'd have someone to tell it to,
but she's waiting for perfection.

I am not perfection,
but I am a storm not to be missed.

We could be lightning, if she'd dare.
But still, we ride the bus to nowhere.

Phoenix

You unwrap the towel from the inside,
you unwrap the towel for me, this time.
And as it drops, we drop into ashes
rolling in and out of rough patches.

We disintegrate completely from torn,
burning together our tongues reborn,
with something destructive to own,
built into the marrow of our bones.

But still, somehow my lips are sore,
and this has never happened before,
propping me up like a broken frame,
you start to unwrap the towel again.

Strings

after The Cure

I was this fragile thing,
left freezing in the snow,
crying for the death of your heart.

I remember you how you used to be.
You never did find that courage to
let it all go.

And now I live in a snowstorm
between angels and avalanches,
running soft through the night.

I see you, always.
But we are too broken to fight.

Pictures of you are all I can feel.
I couldn't hold on to your heart.

Jennifer

Dear *you*.
Who else can I address this to?

From *me.*
Who do I want myself to be?

And what are these words
I find myself writing in between?

That I am an adult now,
and I am building my life?
I've left what was 'home',
and even that was years ago.

I drink now,
even though I said I wouldn't.
But it's sort of a stimulant
and it's easier than therapy.

I take pills to keep my mind sane
my face tame, and my world a better place.
I have tattoos, and scars, and flaws.
I wrote a book that doesn't feel
like poetry anymore.

I have a degree, working multiple jobs
and my stories are published in collections.
And I'd love to tell you all of this,
but with that comes your resurrection.

And I don't know if I have strength for that,
so I'll begin with a letter because I'm scared.
If I never come around,
I won't make peace and that might kill me.

I've climbed mountain height since,
and it would be a shame to fall that far again.
This head vs heart war is my biggest fear,
but stop, take a look at me, I've made it here.

I moved on, and it's my biggest regret,
I moved on, and you're not even dead.

Leather Jacket

I was wearing
my father's leather jacket:
a black cloak
dangling to my ankles,
drowning my skinny arms.

He must have heard
the rush of my tiny feet
splashing around the kitchen:
me becoming breathless,
him becoming blurry.

"Tell you what," he says to me.
"When it fits you, it's yours."
He fishes out my hand
from his own left sleeve,
and we shake on it.

I am wearing
my father's leather jacket:
a black cloak
dangling to my hips,
embracing my stronger arms.

Beans

Beans grinding reminds me of knuckle-busting
back in the schoolyard, conkers shattered
over concrete like these shortcake crumbs.
I counted forty-seven. Someone made a mess.

In black swirl, I wonder how we mourn froth,
and shoot up on the good stuff, our palms
embracing a chipped handle like cracked ice,
and the weight of the world on top.

You're Gorgeous and Petty's *Free Fallin'*
brings me back to life, eyes away
from the boots and back on the prize -
Twitter journal and Instagram therapy.

If we were talking about moods, I'd say
my shoelaces are untied and winking again.
The cheek of it reminds me of a cheap joke,
as bad as the sugar sticking underfoot.

Soon morning turns into night, and the kids
come rolling in for milkshakes and coolers,
easily satisfied with drunken sweet tooths,
already mastering the art of skinny jeans.

The Harvest

Lay me down, to sink in my grave,
to the sound of your disregarded voice,
a seductive lullaby, intended to subdue.
I am the mud and I'm dying, drying
up in the sun of a teenage love.

I no longer claw away at my roots,
in need of air to breathe, and live.
I'm more than happy here, my body
sleeping like rain after a storm,
finally at peace with the earth.

Until the beating of your drums,
harvests me in all of my glory.
My hands resurrect through the dirt,
desperately reaching out for you.
And tonight, we sink here together.

Moonflower

The park bench on Northern Road
is the perfect place for moonflower wander,
at two a.m., listening to slurring stampedes,

of broken footsteps flooding the streets
and shouting in the dark as to why Saturday
will always be the best night of the week.

Here, we could fall in love with the world,
and out of love with everyone in it,
sleeping the days away again.

Through deserted trek, we count shards
of broken glass hidden in blades of grass
casting imagery of the short side of life.

I can say I've seen every side of beautiful,
and I've witnessed every side of ugly
in the short time that I've been alive.

We should let life find us in the darkness
to suck out all the poison nakedly exposed.
And on this park bench, I've seen it all.

Mark, The Wanderer

Enveloped in soft acoustic sounds
as my feet begin to click with the ground.
It's midnight and I'm still walking the town,
seeing if ghosts are still hanging around.

I am so attached to this evening sky,
that my mind just wants to take flight
at speeds in which my body could ignite
and together we'll fall out of the sky tonight.

Stargazing with our backs to a tarmac road,
I am no longer afraid of growing old,
because you make my body implode,
and my lips tremble when you lean in close.

So walk with me, to a place with no name,
your hand in mine, hearts leading the way.
I will wander down any darkened path for you,
as long as you're with me, guiding me through.

Chrysalis

I am not a sociable person.

I am an anti-social butterfly
that never did transform.

But you had the most beautiful wings.
I was mesmerised by the colours,
and the way you moved,

distracting me from my not-so-empty
glass that made home on the
coffee table you never use for coffee.

You were more of a 'whiskey girl'
caught up in a chardonnay world.

And you looked great that night,
so I have no idea why I left.

Making awkward conversation
with you is my favourite thing.
My heart races. My lips sting.

I guess what I'm saying is...
it isn't easy for me to show my wings.

So I avoid all kinds of things
that could hurt me,

or break me.
I am not a social butterfly today.
But I'm happy enough to just be me.

Revival of the Self

There are roads
with destinations
we've never reached,
and everybody sleepwalks

down these streets,
trying locked doors.
If I show you my world,
can I see yours?

Verse isn't something
to view as abstract.
A poem is just another way
for me to breathe.

Loving you is something
to view as abstract.
Even as we find ourselves
wandering the streets,

fighting off shadows
that dominate the concrete.
The moon might be
your only friend tonight.

Hell's looking for a hero
to take the limelight, and
we're all suffering from
heaven's stage-fright,

swimming in dangerous
waters to the surface.
even if it's worth it,
even if the earth is fucked.

Love isn't a topic for poems
when you're hurting, but
finding the source of the pain
is the way forward.

Hospital Bedside

I'm not sure how we got here,
or where I'm going from here.
I don't know how the world is coping
without you, outside of these walls.
I do know, you shouldn't be here.
You should be out in the world
making it better for just being in it.

I also know that I hate the smell
of hand sanitiser these days,
and that every photo of you I find
is now an indestructible treasure.
They only die when I die.

And I know to sing as loud as I can
when I hear your favourite song,
because you're too weak to sing with me.
And this way, I know you'll hear me.

You are a way of the world.
You made everything count
and opened my eyes to see clearly.
Family isn't a law to abide by,
it's a way of life and a choice.

And I choose to hold your hand through this,
feeling stronger and weaker at the same time.
Feeling like a better person and worse.
Feeling relieved at your final breath but hurt.

Like something I've never experienced before.
Like a knife wound through the heart,
I shot out of a dream and I opened my eyes.
At 5.45, from the hospital bedside, goodbye.

The Bluebird

after Charles Bukowski

If there's a bluebird in my heart,
why won't she come out?
Maybe she's too tough for me,
hiding away in her nest,
me begging her, be free, bird.
You have wings, so use them.

If there's a bluebird in my heart,
why won't she come out?
Hiding away in dreams of you,
she revels in the tranquillity,
the solemn, the emptiness.
Sometimes I wonder,
if she's still in there.

If there's a bluebird in my heart,
why won't she come out?
Doesn't she know,
she could suffocate in there?
She could drown in all
my broken promises.

Then her wings flutter,
and I remember why.
The world isn't ready,
and neither is she.
And that's okay.

Woman

Woman,
I barely recognise,
what should I do with my eyes?

I know you know that I'm staring.
I hate that I'm staring.
But you've taken me by surprise.

You cannot fall into my life
looking the way you do
and not expect me to fall, too.

Alright,
I've already fallen.
I'll admit it.

Heavy and hard,
quick and messy,
painfully and beautifully.

Now, it could be the whiskey and ice.
It could be how you look tonight.
It could be how you're dressed tonight.

It could be the patterns of my mind
playing tricks on me tonight.
It could be a death by sight.

We are a modern love, my love.

No games or rules to remember.
Just the bloke at the bar wondering
what I meant when I said...

It'd be pointless to give you my number.

But that's another story.
Woman, I like our story.
I never want it to end.

Even a 'happily ever after'
doesn't appeal to me much anymore.
I like the pain that comes with the plot,
because I love how you make me feel things.

Woman,
forgive my paralytic, apologetic response
of wandering through the dancefloor

to find a source of pathetic, aesthetic ways
of looking at the world,
stripped down to naked bones.

You are everything I have tonight,
and you're everything I don't want.
And so, I just can't help myself.

Woman, I barely recognise you,
when you're leaning in that closely.

You've switched your eyes for passion,

and it's a contagious kind of passion.
That's my favourite thing about you.

God, I hope he makes you feel beautiful.
I know I'll never have that privilege.
Or, would you be happy that I'm staring?

From this section of the bar,
I've mentally labelled safe zone.
I'll let you in, but I won't set foot out of it.

I'm terrified to make a twat of myself.

Woman, I barely recognise myself.
The dance-floor brings out the real me
and that scares me to death.

You make me fear living,
because it's dangerous.

You make me love danger,
because it's living.

Woman, I don't even know your name,
but you broke my safe zone with your danger.

And for that,
I cannot thank you enough.

Printed in Great Britain
by Amazon